fONTENAY
the Abbey and the Vale

TEXT
FRANÇOIS AYNARD

PHOTOGRAPHS
NICOLAS BRUANT

ENGLISH TRANSLATION
LINDA ASHER

«*To grasp Fontenay in what makes for its meaning and the force of its beauty, one must approach it step by step, by its forested paths, in October rain, through its brambles and ruts.*»

GEORGES DUBY

CONTENTS

A New setting
FOR FONTENAY

interview with the landscape designer

Fontenay's garden has been completely redesigned... to bring new life to the place, and to set off the Abbey as one sets off a jewel.

Peter Holmes, landscape designer : he completely reconceived the Abbey's garden.

giving the garden sense

THE LANDSCAPE GARDENER, PETER HOLMES, did not take his inspiration from the past, from the garden as it was centuries ago; he did not seek out the original drawings for ideas. And yet, looking at the gardens after the fact, he saw that certain of his ideas were already at work in the 18th century. Probably because they seemed obviously right for the place.

THE GARDEN, ALL IN HARMONIES OF BLUE AND WHITE, has immediate charm. Yet it was very rationally designed. Nothing was left to chance. "The first thing I did was work out the basic structure, a structure that would make some sense. Only then did I consider the plants. For me, a garden is like a house whose furniture is the plants--and they may be laid out well or poorly."

GIVING THE GARDEN sense means first of all looking to harmonize the life of the owners in residence at Fontenay with the comfort of visitors. For the latter, Peter Holmes sought to create a space without barriers where they could move about freely. Only the flowerbeds themselves function as boundaries. They are designed to be seen from both the public and the private sides at once. "I wanted to do away with most of the signs saying 'private', and have the traffic pattern emerge naturally."

a stage set for the buildings

LIKE ALL LANDSCAPE DESIGNERS worthy of the name, Peter Holmes dislikes gardens where the whole thing is visible at first glance; he has us discover the wonders of the place little by little, at each successive bend in "his" garden.

"In planting trees between the dovecote and the abbots' residence, for instance, my point was to conceal the façade from the gaze of the viewer coming into the Abbey complex. He discovers it as the path turns."

THE SPACE AS A WHOLE is made up of several small gardens, all of them different. "Each bed has its own purpose within this fully thought-out landscape: either to interrupt a line, or to bring out the qualities of some building."

THE COLOURS OF THE BEDDING PLANTS were chosen with equal care. Yellow shrubs at the waterfall, to provide a look of sunshine in the middle of winter, which is extremely cold at Fontenay. Blue and white flowers for the center beds, amid feathery foliage to respect the colour harmony. "If you notice, in these long beds the shrubs are set out architecturally: the tallest ones along the center, the others growing shorter out to the edge."

E.D.

PETER HOLMES :

"A GARDEN IS LIKE A HOUSE
WHOSE FURNITURE IS THE PLANTS."

Right page :
Fontenay's park,
east side.

HISTORY

cîteaux, the "new monastery"

The Cistercian revolution in Western monastic life was a return to the spirit and the letter of the New Testament. The strict application of St Benedict's Rule was the mechanism for the Cistercian ideal.

religious men in quest of the absolute

Left page and above : September 21, 1947 : celebrating Fontenay's 800th anniversary.

THE "NUOVUM MONASTERIUM" OF CÎTEAUX, the monastery that was the founding mother of the Cistercian order, did not appear out of nowhere ("ex nihilo") in the late eleventh century. It was born of decades of discontent and reflection. After a thousand years of Christianity, its followers were rebelling against deviations from the earliest Christian ideal and against the heresies. In solitude and poverty they would connect afresh with the origins of Christianity, and to achieve this they determined to invent a new monastic life. They rejected the model of the rich Cluny-order abbeys, choosing instead the "horrible vast solitudes" (as St Bernard called them) of the forest, and living there away from the world like the desert fathers, in strict obedience to the Rule of St Benedict.

IN 1070, a group of hermits gathered in the Collan Forest, near Tonnerre in Burgundy. The Abbot Robert, from the Provins Priory, soon joined them. The little community moved in 1075 to the Molesme forest to found a monastery there, in which the future St Bruno and the British churchman Stephen Harding would also spend some time. But the reformers were soon caught up again by the world they had fled: the flow of donations to the monastery, and its growing wealth, came to stand in the way of monastic poverty.

A FEW OF THE PIONEERS decided to leave the community with Abbot Robert. The men went to the papal legate in Lyons, Archbishop Hugues : their plan was to establish a new monastery for "stricter observance of St Benedict's Rule than they had kept hitherto." Their request was granted; the new community was established on marshland covered with bulrushes (*cistels* in French, the likely source of the name "Cîteaux"). The new monastery was born. By two centuries later, Cîteaux had given birth to a thousand other "Cistercian" settlements in Europe!

isolation, poverty and self-sufficiency

THE EARLY CISTERCIANS were fleeing the world. Away from cities and chateaux, they founded their abbeys in remote areas, whenever possible in harsh inaccessible valleys. The monks were to live in silence and poverty. No rich garments : their habit was woven of undyed, ecru-coloured wool, which led to the expression "white monks" to describe Cistercians. No rich foodstuffs–meat was forbidden in the early period–and no hearth to warmth in the conventual halls, despite winters cold enough to crack rock. The monks and their abbot slept on plain mats in a large common dormitory.

> "IN LIFE WE MUST
> SEEK PEACE :
> PEACE WITH GOD,
> PEACE WITH NEIGHBOR,
> PEACE WITH OURSELF."
> *BERNARD OF CLAIRVAUX*

THIS REJECTION OF LUXURY and of the superfluous is evident in the architecture of Cistercian structures, whose beauty still amazes us nine centuries later ; the churches, cloisters, refectories, all the conventual buildings of the abbeys of the Cîteaux order–when not remodeled, of course–are characterized by great sobriety.

THE WHITE MONKS pray and read the sacred texts. But they also do physical labor, and this is a fundamental feature of the Cistercian project. Separate from the world, but without dependence on the world! They provide for their own community's needs. The Rule of S\ Benedict is explicit on this point : "If possible, the monastery shall be organized in such fashion that everything necessary–the water, the milling, the garden–shall exist inside the monastery, and the various trades shall be practiced there, so that the monks are not forced to reach outside, which would not befit their souls."

MONKS FIRST ESTABLISHING an abbey had the enormous job of clearing and draining the terrain. Once nature was brought to heel, the Cistercians did remarkable work in agriculture and livestock-raising, as well as in industrial production (iron, tiles, glass, ceramics, et cetera). Thanks to the labour of lay brothers and serfs–though the use of paid workers was theoretically forbidden in the early days of the order–the abbeys' estates prospered. Several of them spun off separate production centers (called "granges"), sometimes at a distance from the monastery, and goods produced there were sold commercially.

*Right page :
church doorway.*

The swarming of the cistercian monasteries

THE CISTERCIAN ORDER underwent great expansion throughout the twelfth century. After some years, the Cîteaux Abbey could no longer accommodate all the new recruits seeking to join it. Colonies of monks broke off from the mother-abbey to found new monasteries : La Ferté (in 1113), Pontigny (in 1114), Morimond and Clairvaux (in 1115). At the instigation of St Bernard, once a monk at Cîteaux and then the first abbot of Clairvaux, those four daughters of the mother-abbey in turn generated new abbeys. By 1200, there were five hundred thirty Cistercian monasteries scattered throughout Europe.

AS NEW SITES WERE ESTABLISHED, the abbeys as a group came to constitute a veritable monastic order. In 1114, Stephen Harding had promulgated a Rule to unify them. Each abbey could elect its own abbot, but was supervised by its mother-abbey. The monasteries had equal rank, and would each year gather in full assembly (the Chapter General) at Cîteaux to vote on decisions concerning the order.

WITH THE 13TH CENTURY, the expansion rate of Cistercian abbeys slowed. Strict observance of the Rule began to ease after 1220 ; the Chapter General lifted most of its prohibitions.
The Cistercian abbeys began to levy tithes. Noblemen could now be buried within the churches, a practice which had been forbidden earlier. The monasteries grew very rich and no longer looked much different from the feudal estates. In a sense, the monks fell victim to their own hard work and their genius for organizing production.

IN THE SIXTEENTH CENTURY, THE SPREADING PRACTICE OF "commendation" sped the decline of the Cistercian abbeys ; abbots were now named by the king rather than elected by the monks. Property management and discipline grew extremely lax.

It would be futile to blame the decline on some internal distortion of the Cistercian system. On the contrary, it was the very perfection and loftiness of that ideal that could not stand against the vicissitudes of history over the long term.

Bernard, or god's knight

Bernard, the abbot of Clairvaux, was the dominant figure of his time, through his writings, his preaching, and his tireless activity at the heart of twelfth-century society. Whether one admires or disputes him, the aura of this champion of church reform shines still.

S^T Bernard's extraordinary personality and work had a powerful effect on his own time and on the centuries to follow. However, he should not be credited–as certain overenthusiastic hagiographers have done–with founding Cîteaux Abbey; that had already existed for fourteen years when Bernard joined it. It is also incorrect to speak of "St Bernard's Rule;" the saint only advocated the return to St Benedict's Rule. The term that best describes this church father is "reformer."

Throughout his life (1090-1153), Bernard of Clairvaux laboured to reconstruct a Church thoroughly dedicated to the glory of God. In his view, the best way to accomplish this mission would be monastic vocation and the return to Bible study.

The monastery over the military

Bernard was born in 1090 to a noble Burgundy family, the son of Tescelin de Châtillon and Aleth de Montbard. This future Abbot of Clairvaux spent his childhood in the family chateau at Fontaine-les-Dijon, before going off to the school run by the canons of Châtillon-sur-Seine. There he began Bible study, and came to know the great authors of Roman antiquity. An aristocrat, Bernard was also highly literate, as shown by the elegant language of his writings («Sermons on the Canticle», «On the Love of God», «On the Degrees of Humility and Pride», «Consideration», and other works). His artistic temperament inclined him more toward poetry than dialectic. He was a sensitive, delicate young man, but neither mawkish nor sentimental. Frail of constitution, rather sickly, he nonetheless overflowed with energy and vigor. His courage might have drawn him to choose a military career, his uncommon intelligence might have taken him into the loftiest functions of church heirarchy–but the young nobleman determined instead to quit the world to serve God. He entered the Cîteaux Abbey at the age of twenty-two, bringing with him his uncle, his cousins, his friends–a total of some thirty men. "His body emaciated by

"GOD'S AFFAIRS ARE MY AFFAIRS; NOTHING THAT CONCERNS THEM IS ALIEN TO ME."

BERNARD OF CLAIRVAUX

fasting and by the hardships of the wilderness, and his pallor, give him an almost spiritual quality ; the mere sight of the man persuades his listeners before he even opens his mouth," writes the historian Wibald Stavelot.

Both a mystic and a man of action

IN 1115, BERNARD SET OUT TO ESTABLISH THE CLAIRVAUX Abbey, but he was to spend only about a third of his life in that monastery. Such is the paradox of this great mystic who had chosen to withdraw from the world. Bernard went on to involve himself personally in all the major events of his time, whenever he felt that his ideal for the Church was at stake. "God's affairs are my affairs," he said ; "nothing that concerns them is alien to me." The commitment that forced him out onto the highways of Europe was not impelled by a thirst for personal power: Bernard remained merely the abbot of Clairvaux throughout his whole life. At most he might be accused of occasionally seeking advancement for certain men from his abbey, but that was because he believed in their merit ; it was individuals that interested him, not institutions. When, in the schism that split the Western church between 1130 and 1138, he supported Innocent II for pope over Anacletus II, it was on grounds of Innocent's personal merit.

IN THE POLITICAL REALM, Bernard wielded a large influence as well. He gave unstintingly of his advice, and from far and wide came appeals for him to step in and resolve conflicts. Bernard exhorted the powerful to justice and peace. He condemned luxury and constantly urged the primacy of the common good. Doctrinal conflicts found him involved in the front lines. His theological "dispute over universals" with the monk Abelard, whom he persuaded the Council of Sens to condemn in 1140, has come down to posterity.

The failure of the second crusade

BUT NOT ALL THE SAINT'S UNDERTAKINGS WERE SUCCESSFUL. On March 31st, 1146, he preached the Second Crusade at Vézelay, and roused the crowds to fervour. Then he journeyed through France and the Holy Roman Empire to gather support from the powerful. But the military expedition turned to disaster, and the

> **"WHAT IS GOD ?
> HE IS LENGTH, BREADTH,
> HEIGHT AND DEPTH."**
> *BERNARD OF CLAIRVAUX*

Second Crusade finally collapsed in 1148. Bernard would be blamed for the defeat, and he grew embittered.

KNIGHT OF THE FAITH, "a man obsessed with Christ and His Church," to quote Dom Jean Leclercq's phrase (in *Saint Bernard and the Cistercian Spirit*), Bernard certainly belongs to the tradition of "hard-liners" utterly dedicated to a cause. For this reason he may either fascinate or exasperate. But we should be careful not to interpret the man's uncompromising austerity as hard-heartedness. Bernard's writings testify to a compassion for human frailty. He never felt himself to be above such frailty.

St Benedict's Rule applied to the letter

•*The Italian monk Benedict of Nursia* (born about 480; died between 546 and 550) was the author of the Rule that codified Western monastic life and that bears his name: the "Regula Sancti Benedicti," or "Rule of St Benedict." The early Cistercians wished to live by that rule as strictly as possible, in contrast to the Cluny monks who had gradually moved away from it. St Benedict drew his inspiration from the "Rule of the Master," an anonymous text supposedly written near Rome in the early sixth century. The monk also quoted Pacôme, Augustine,

Cassianus and the Bible. The Rule of St Benedict consists of seventy-three chapters with a prologue. It deals both with the spiritual discipline for living in the Good, and with concrete aspects of community living.

•*In the spiritual realm,* the Rule demands absolute obedience to the abbot, respect for silence, and humility. Labour is essential, be it manual or intellectual, for "idleness is the enemy of the soul." The monks must possess nothing of their own, and must "work hard to shrive the monastery of that vice of property."

•*In the practical realm,* the Rule laid out directives on a monk's dress, on food and sleep, on the treatment of ailing monks, on appropriate punishments, the election of the abbot, and the reception of guests.

The sequence of holy offices and the reciting of psalms are also meticulously codified. Although it was not entirely original, the Rule of St Benedict prospered because of the humanity that imbues it, its advocacy of good sense and moderation.

The birth of fontenay, second daughter-house of clairvaux

The Fontenay adventure began one fine autumn morning in the year 1118. Under the guidance of St Bernard, a band of pioneers set up a makeshift camp in a marshy hollow near a hermitage.

AFTER THE FOUNDING OF CÎTEAUX ABBEY (1098) and Clairvaux (1115), the third generation of Cistercian abbeys was born with the creation of Trois-Fontaines in 1118. The indefatigable Bernard of Clairvaux went on with his labours, guiding handfuls of men into tangled wilderness to set up new communities remote from the world. On October 26, 1118, according to legend accompanied by twelve monks, Bernard set out from Clairvaux. The men walked west. A few leagues from Montbard they stopped amid the Grand Jailly woods, at the site called "Chastellum".

Two hermits, the brothers Martin and Milon, lived there. Their hermitage was built on a rock and surrounded by walls, at the far end of the St Bernard pond. Bernard was rather at home here ; the Chateau of Touillon, a few leagues upstream, belonged to his uncle Gaudry. The abbot of Clairvaux made his decision ; the valley would be the birthplace of the new abbey.

"fontanetum" : a float upon springs

FOR THE NEXT TWELVE YEARS, the little colony of monks lived clustered around the "chastellum" overlooking the pond. Bernard went back to Clairvaux. The pioneers were joined by other monks, and the Cistercian settlement was soon too small. The colony moved south of the pond, to the crossing of that hollow and another valley now called the Vale of Fontenay. The Abbey had found its final location. The land was granted by Etienne de Bagé, Bishop of Autun, and by Bernard's maternal uncle Rainard de Montbard.

The place was marshy, full of springs and subsurface streams: silent waters welling up on all sides. This is probably the origin of Fontenay's name : Fontanetum, "afloat upon springs."

AN ENORMOUS TASK LAY BEFORE THE MONKS. They had to make the land habitable, contain the springs and channel them. The first project to be completed was the construction of two dikes that still stand to the north and east of the Abbey. Gradually, the area was put in condition to allow the monks a self-sufficient existence.

Building the church

CONSTRUCTION OF THE ABBEY-CHURCH began in 1139 and was largely completed less than ten years later. The great vessel of the nave has lasted through more than eight centuries of history, and seems destined for eternity. Perfection of volumes, purity of forms–it calls up St Bernard's reflection : "What is God? He is length, breadth, height and depth."

"THE SUN BRINGS
LIFE TO THE AUSTERE
BARENESS OF
CISTERCIAN
ARCHITECTURE,
THE WAY GOD'S
LIGHT SPREADS
GRACE THROUGH
THE SIMPLICITY-
LOVING SOUL
OF THE MONKS."
PIERRE-GILLES GIRAULT

*The transept of
Fontenay church*

THERE IS NO CHRONICLE OF THE CONSTRUCTION OF FONTENAY church. We only know that it was consecrated on October 21, 1147, by Pope Eugene III, in the presence of eight cardinals, Bernard of Clairvaux, many other Cistercian abbots and three hundred monks.

Detail from the tomb of Evrard of Norwich.

The patron of fontenay

THE BUILDERS' EXPRESSION OF FAITH was underwritten by a patron, the English bishop Evrard of Norwich. A victim of religious persecution, Evrard left his bishopric and took refuge in the peace of the Vale of Fontenay. He used his enormous fortune to finance the construction of the church and of the Abbey as a whole.

The construction site must have employed hundreds of monks and lay brothers from Fontenay and other abbeys, as well as peasants from the area, even though the use of salaried labour was theoretically forbidden. First the stone to lay the foundations had to be quarried near the S¹ Bernard pond. For years, men loaded carts and wound winches while stonecutters wielded their shears.

SAINT BERNARD MUST CERTAINLY HAVE VISITED the Fontenay construction site. He would have refueled the fervour of all those men, which must often falter before the enormous project. Could they have known that they were building, with makeshift means, the perfect forms that a Le Corbusier would echo eight centuries later?

seven centuries of monastery life : 1130-1790

The Fontenay Abbey, like the Cistercian order itself, flourished from the thirteenth to the mid-fifteenth century, when it began a decline that continued until the French Revolution. That event put an end to six hundred seventy-two years of monastery life.

ALTHOUGH THE RENOWNED BERNARD had overseen its birth, Fontenay later harboured no great figure among its monks, nor was it at the centre of any historical or intellectual activity.

It was involved in history only unwillingly--through being plundered several times ; in 1359, by the English; in 1419 by the Robeurs ; in 1590 and 1595 by the Catholic League, the Landsknechts, the Burgundians and the Armagnacs.*

A Royal Abbey with Broad privileges

ON THE OTHER HAND, Fontenay was an abbey of the first order in terms of its sizeable domain and of the rights it enjoyed. Kings, princes, dukes and lords all competed to grant their favors to Fontenay. In 1250, Hugues IV, Duke of Burgundy, placed the Abbey's forests under his protection on the condition that he should have exclusive hunting rights there. In 1259, Saint Louis exempted the monastery from all taxes on land and water use within his States. Fontenay became an "abbey-royal" in 1269. In the early 16th century, Charles VIII took the Abbey under his protection. Louis XII gave the monks permission to raise fortress walls and turrets for defense against invaders. Father Corbolin declares: "Such protections and favors granted Fontenay at various periods by several kings made it an abbey-royal not by origin but by adoption. That is why it put a fleur-de-lis in its coat of arms."

IN THE SPIRITUAL REALM, too, Fontenay enjoyed significant privileges. The monks could elect their abbot, even in an abbey elsewhere, as was the case at Flavigny and Pontigny. The Abbot of Fontenay had the right to carry the pontifical insignia (mitre, cross, ring) and to give the papal blessing. The Abbey was not subject to inspection or jurisdiction by the regional bishop, nor could it be forced to sell its holdings. It could exercise the right of asylum not only within its monastery walls but on its

*Above :
the Fontenay
arms above
the entryway.*

* Our source here is the Monograph on the Abbey of Fontenay, Clairvaux's Second Daughter, published in 1882 by the Abbé Corbolin, priest at nearby Marmagne.

farmsteads as well. Fontenay was also exempt from paying tithes on its lands, whether they were cultivated directly by the monks, or indirectly.

IN THE JUDICIAL REALM, the abbot of Fontenay handled all matters of justice within its lands, regardless of whether they had come into the Abbey's possession by clearing, by purchase, or by donation. Acting for the abbot, the cellarer of the convent was the one who dispensed justice, including sentencing to the gibbet, prison, fines, or sometimes exile.

fontenay's prosperity

THROUGH A SUCCESSION OF GIFTS, Fontenay quickly came to cover a vast area, reaching beyond the vale that today's visitor crosses to approach the Abbey. Its domain stretched as far as Nesles, Planay, Laignes, Lucenay-le-Duc, and so on. Corbolin calculates that "hard-working Fontenay" had three hundred monks and lay-brothers in the thirteenth and fourteenth centuries. Most of them lived outside the monastery walls in the granges, priories, or villages of the domain.

Aside from the crops, the monks raised troops of cattle and sheep. They also farmed fish, and the Fontenay trout were famous. The monks had constructed four ponds, to channel the streams, but also to drive the mills. And water power was utilized by the ironworks built on the locale in the l2th century.

SEVERAL CHURCHES DEPENDED FROM FONTENAY, (Planay, Fresnes, and such...) and the Abbey had "Little Fontenays" at Tonnerre, Autun, Pommard, Semur, Montbard, and Dijon. The one in Dijon, near the Prefecture, served as residence for the abbots when in town to pay court to the kings and dukes, or when they were delegated to represent the clergy at the Estates of Burgundy parliament.

Above :
the waterfall
supplying power
to the forge.

"wherever the wind blows, to fontenay money flows"

UNTIL THE 14TH CENTURY, princely gifts and the abundant labour force of its serfs would support the Abbey's prosperity.

Corbolin writes that the Abbey had attained "a level of wealth truly remarkable for a daughter-abbey." The Burgundian proverb, "Wherever the wind blows, to Fontenay money flows," could apply, says the author, who reckons that the Abbey collected income in at least a hundred twenty Burgundy villages.

LIKE MANY OTHER ABBEYS, FONTENAY DOUBTLESS FELL VICTIM TO ITS OWN SUCCESS. The monks' too-great wealth soon exceeded their ability to manage it. In the late Middle Ages, a new world was emerging with the growth of the cities ; the lay brothers left the countryside for the town, serfs switched manorhouses, tenant farmers quit paying their rent.

By the l6th century, the number of Fontenay monks had shrunk to fifty.

The Decline

IT IS GENERALLY CONCEDED THAT THE SYSTEM OF "COMMENDATION" is what started the Abbey's process of decline. Fontenay came under such rule in 1547. From then on, the abbots of Fontenay were named by the king, rather than elected by the community of monks. The administration of the monastery lost a good deal of its rigour with that change.

The commendatory abbots were often responsible for several abbeys at once. Charles de Sauvebeuf, at age fifteen, was in charge of eight abbeys.

These new leaders no longer exerted any spiritual authority over the community, and often sent representatives to collect the revenues. Certain abbots even carried off books from the library.

IN THE 18TH CENTURY, lots of visits by the abbots of Trois-Fontaines and Clairvaux described the collapse of the Rule at Fontenay. In 1777, Pierre VI, Abbot of Clairvaux, issued an order prohibiting gambling, hunting, and the presence of women in the monastery.

ON JANUARY 13, 1790, THE NATIONAL ASSEMBLY OF THE NEW REVOLUTIONARY French Republic decreed that all holdings of religious communities were now the property of the Nation. On October 29, 1790, the last eight monks of Fontenay left the place forever, 672 years after the founding of the Abbey.

Below :
the residence built
during the 18ᵗʰ century,
for the commendatory
Abbots.

visiting fontenay

Around the cloister

Centered around the cloister, Fontenay's conventual halls are laid out along the plan particular to Cistercian monasteries.

The church

THE FONTENAY CHURCH-ABBEY is one of the oldest Cistercian structures, and in perfectly preserved state. As was the custom, the church is oriented toward the east, and located on the highest point of the terrain.

Its façade is completely bare, broken only by two buttresses and seven windows. The original porch was demolished in the eighteenth century, but one can detect the corbels that used to support its stringpiece beam.

Step through the portal, and you enter into a universe of silence and beauty. The Romanesque church of Fontenay is majestic–66 meters long and 16.70 meters high–but not overwhelming like some cathedrals.

THE CHURCH IS CONSTRUCTED ALONG THE LINES OF A BASILICA, in the form of a Latin cross; it has a nave with two side-aisles, a transept, and a flat chevet. The transept is flanked on either side by two rectangular chapels. It is a model of Burgundian Romanesque architecture.

Nothing distracts the eye, in accordance with the wishes of St Bernard and the Chapter General of the Cîteaux order.

The latter had ruled in 1134 that the windows should be of clear glass, with neither cross nor staining. Fontenay's leaded windows were copied from those in the Obazine Abbey in Corrèze. In that same spirit of simplicity, the capitals are minimally sculpted, with just a very light relief of leaves. Only a few capitals of the separation arches along the side-aisles are decorated with half-round bands.

THE GREAT SPACE OF THE CHURCH NAVE is spanned by a pointed barrel-vault on joists supported by cruciform pillars. The vault has an ogive shape made of two arcs intersecting.

Left page :
the nave of
the abbey-church.

The side-aisles are formed of a series of vaults on an axis perpendicular to the nave. This feature, which is found in a certain number of eleventh- and twelfth-century Burgundian buildings, offers an advantage ; the pressure of the large vault is countered by the thrust of the lateral ones.

At either side of the nave, the row of eight low bays made for as many chapels–that is, sixteen in all–where important figures were buried. The second chapel on the epistle side was for the Dukes of Burgundy.

The transept with its broken-barrel vault lies much lower than the nave. The same is true for the sanctuary (mistakenly called "choir"), which is square and is two steps higher. The difference in levels is compensated by a rear wall with five window openings in it.

The Fontenay church is characterized by a one-level elevation, and the only windows are a single row in the outer walls of the aisles (as at Thoronet and Bonmont), so that the nave is lighted indirectly.

Far left :
the door to
the cloister

⊞ *The monks would go into the church to take part in services and masses, but also to pray in the course of the day. They were not permitted to read there, however ; the oratory was strictly reserved for prayer. The nave, which is now bare and of a single piece, was originally divided into three very distinct sections. The first choir (or "monks' choir") was used by the monks and the novices. The stalls where the monks sat were arranged in a U against the pillars. A "jubé" or rood-screen separated the intersection of the transept from the rest of the nave. Traces of it can still be seen on the two first pillars, and Gothic-style fragments (from the mid-13th century) have been collected. The next choir was used by the sick and the elderly monks, while the third choir was for the lay brothers, who entered the church by a special door, now walled over, on the south side-aisle. At the very foot of the church, the Abbey's salaried workers, and outsiders, could stand, but only for certain special celebrations.*

The Virgin of Fontenay: a Medieval Masterpiece

In the north section of the transept, the sculpture of the Virgin Mary is an extraordinary example of Burgundian statuary of the late thirteenth century. The Fontenay church was dedicated to the Virgin Mary, in honor of S' Bernard's devotion to her. Mary, with a crown on her head, carries the Infant Jesus on her left arm, and her right holds a sceptre now broken.

The statue was sold during the Revolution to a resident of Touillon for six francs, and for over two centuries it stood exposed to the weather in the village cemetery. In 1929 it was bought back for 50 000 F by the Beaux Arts ministry together with the Abbey's owner who restored it, and it was agreed that the statue would never leave Fontenay again.

The Tombs

MOST OF THE TOMBSTONES of the Abbey's benefactors had been lifted away by the monks themselves in the 18th century (and sometimes even used as building material!). They are now set around the sanctuary.

The most imposing tomb stands on the south side. A true mausoleum from the outset, it is made up of a modern pedestal bearing the reclining figures of a knight and his wife. The man's feet rest on two lions, and the woman's on two greyhounds. The helmeted knight is wearing armor, and his sword is partly traced with the coat of arms of the Mello de Bourgogne family, aristocrats originally from Picardy who lived in Burgundy in the late 14th century.

AMONG THE EIGHT LARGE GRAVESTONES that now ring the church sanctuary, note that of Evrard, Bishop of Norwich, who financed the construction of the Abbey-church. Evrard is represented with the ornaments of his status as bishop, his crossed hands gripping the pastoral staff on his chest. A handsome altar-screen stands against the wall of the church's apse. This whole assemblage was probably part of the main altar of the church. It was badly damaged by use as flooring in the 18th century. Its reliefs show various Biblical scenes, such as the Nativity, the Crucifixion, and the Resurrection.

The Dormitory

Above :
details from
the tombstone
of the Chevalier
Mello d'Epoisses
and his wife.

IN THE RIGHT ARM OF THE TRANSEPT (the south end) a stairway leads up to the monks' dormitory. That staircase was remodeled when the earth was banked up around the church, and the banister was added.

The dormitory has a magnificent wooden ceiling structure, dating from the 16th century, that resembles the overturned hull of a ship. It is of oak, not chestnut as has often been said. Three great arches, discovered beneath the roughcast mortar of the eastern wall, indicate that the dormitory extended toward the garden.

The original flooring, probably unglazed tile, is gone.

The Rule of S' Benedict stipulates that all the monks must sleep in the same room. A hundred beds stood along the walls, and, at the center of the hall were horizontal bars ("pertica") for hanging bedding or clothes. The monks slept fully dressed, on simple mats with a thin coverlet to protect them from the very harsh winter cold. But by the late Middle Ages, true bedrooms were built.

At Fontenay, in the 18th century, the pryor was housed in a real apartment at the southernmost end of the building.

The staircase a visitor climbs from the transept was used by the monks to attend night services. During the day they used another one, at the far end of the dormitory.

Below :
the 15th century
structure ceiling
in dormitory.

The Habit Makes the Monk

Chapter 55 of the Rule of St Benedict is given over to a monk's clothing. In temperate climates, this included a hooded cowl, a tunic, a scapular–smock or overall–for working , stockings, and shoes. Simplicity and poverty were required : "The monks must not be concerned either as to colour or crude quality in these several items; they shall be taken as they exist in the neighborhood, and as cheaply as they can be acquired."

The early Cistercians followed these recommendations to the letter, in reaction against the luxury displayed by some Cluny monks who dressed in furs and fine linens. They also wore a belt with a knife attached to it. They owned two pairs of shoes: leather work-boots for the day and a kind of felt slippers for night. Each monk had two identical outfits. When he had to travel as a representative of the Order, he was given a tunic and cowl of better quality.

the cloister

A SMALL DOOR FROM THE CHURCH lets out onto the cloister ; the heart of the monastery. This Romanesque marvel has remained intact since the twelfth century, whereas the cloisters of Cîteaux and Clairvaux no longer exist.

The four galleries surrounding the cloister court form a rectangle of thirty-six by thirty-eight meters. A gallery contains eight bays, each opening onto the garden through an archivolte set on pillars. In some of these, the usual tympanum and coffered base are absent, to give access into the courtyard. The whole gives off a sense of homogeneity, despite the great variety in the pillars and columns. On the extremely simple capitals there recur the motifs of leaves seen in the church, but with a few entwined ribbon-bands as well. The pavement in the south gallery is the only old one.

▦ *The cloister galleries gave access to every room while still offering shelter from sun or rain. But it was also an area for very particular activities, religious or practical. The east gallery opened directly onto the church and connected with the chapter house. Near that door was an "armarium" where books were kept. Reading ("lectio divina") was scheduled for specific hours of the day, but when they had a free moment, the monks could also sit and read on a coffer-bench in the cloister.*

The gallery backing onto the church was used for the "collatio," in which the monks would listen to a reading before the compline service. Also held there was the weekly religious ceremony of the washing of feet, in Christ's memory.

On the far side, the south gallery was used for practical activities, with ready access to the refectory and the kitchens. In Cistercian abbeys, the washbasin was located in front of that wing (or within the gallery). In its broad hollow the monks could wash their hands and feet; they shaved there too, and barbered their tonsures. Fontenay's washbasin is destroyed, but excavations have uncovered its foundations. The renowned 19th-century architect Viollet-le-Duc designed a reconstruction.

And finally the west gallery ran along the lay-brothers' building and closed off the cloister court.

Above :
Cloister capitals.

View of the cloister
in snow.

Left page :
the south gallery of
the cloister.

The Lay Brothers : they had no "access to the chapter"

The Lay brothers constituted the most sizeable group in the Cistercian monasteries. After a probation period, they did take vows, but they were never permitted to become choir monks afterwards. These lay brothers had their own refectory and dormitory on the west side of the cloister. They had no "access to the chapter"--that is, neither a doorway to it, nor the right to participate in a discussion--but from the cloister they could hear what was being said inside the hall. They did not take part in the holy services, except on Sundays and feast days. Coming from the peasant class in contrast to the Cistercian monks who were aristocrats, they were assigned to the physical duties within the Abbey and to agricultural work in the fields outside. The lay brothers have often been compared to ordinary domestic servants, but founding father Stephen Harding's "Charter of Charity" asserts : "Equal to the monks, they share our possessions, both spiritual and temporal."

Near left :
keystones.

Left page :
the chapter
house.

The chapter house

THE CLOISTER'S EAST GALLERY connected by a handsome vaulted arcade to a vast hall: the capitulary chamber or "chapter house". That room also looked onto the cloister through two round-arched windows on either side of the door. Fontenay's chapter house has a ceiling of groined vaults; originally there were three such bays. The easternmost one was destroyed, but its support pillars can still be seen embedded in the exterior wall.

The hall's elegant, sober architecture indicates the importance of these rooms in Cistercian abbeys. It was in fact the room where the monks gathered each morning, and where the notion of community took on its full meaning. Each day, an excerpt or a chapter of the Rule of St Benedict was read there, which gave the room its name. The monks would sit on benches along the walls, facing the abbot seated against the east wall. At the close of the reading, the abbot would comment on the chosen chapter.

The two windows onto the cloister were not glassed, so that on certain occasions the lay brothers could listen to what was being said in the hall. In the course of the chapter session, the monks would also confess their faults ("the culpa chapter") and the abbot would decide what penalty to levy: fasting, exclusion from church, or corporal punishment. The perpetrators of serious crimes, like theft or rebellion, might be put in a dungeon.

The chapter meetings were also used for practical matters such as the organization of the workday and the assignment of tasks. It was the place for reporting news from other abbeys (deaths, regulations, elections, and so on) and for reading letters from the Pope and from other eminent figures. Lastly, the election of a new abbot of the community would be held in the chapter house.

A Monk's Day : Prayer, Labour, Reading

A Cistercian monk's day was entirely contained between sunrise and sunset. The Rule of St Benedict provided a general framework, with the details laid out by the statutes of the Chapters-General of the Order.

Day after day, the monk's schedule was unchanging; it varied only by the seasons. It was spent at three activities : prayer, the divine reading (lectio divina), and manual labour. Any "free time" was given over to the chapter meeting, to meals, sleep, and bodily care.

The main activity was prayer, that is, the celebration of the "opus Dei" (God's handiwork). Seven services were celebrated between sunrise and sunset : lauds at dawn; prime at sunrise ; terce ; sext at noon ; none ; vespers ; compline before bed. Then there were the vigil service at around two in the morning and a daily mass between 8 and 9 a.m.

In winter, the monks slept longer, but took only one meal, instead of the two of summertime.

Sundays and feast days, the monks did not work, and the physical tasks were replaced by the "lectio divina."

the monks' hall

LEAVING THE CHAPTER HOUSE, you enter a large chamber continuous with it. It measures thirty meters, and is capped by twelve pointed vaults that form two naves of six bays each. This was the monks' hall, a vast room which occurs in all Cistercian abbeys and which was put to a great variety of uses. It may have been partitioned, and probably one of its sections was occupied by the copyists, for there was no particular space assigned to manuscript work in Cistercian abbeys.

Food : bread and the Bible

St Benedict's Rule forbade meat for the monks, except for those who were ill. The mainstay of the diet was bread, baked in the Abbey's ovens and dealt out at the rate of a loaf a day per person. Starting in the 14th century, everyone could eat meat. Each meal (one a day in winter, two in summer and on Sundays) was made up of two cooked dishes, supplemented by fruits and vegetables when available. The Rule authorized one "hémine", about a quarter-liter, of wine a day for each person. The meals in the refectory were to be consumed in silence, and the monks would listen to the reading of a Bible passage.

the heating room

ALONG THE RIGHT-HAND WALL of the monks' hall is a small door into a little room that also connects with the south gallery of the cloister. Two chimney flues show that this must have been the heating room. From outside in the cloister courtyard, a visitor can see two 12th-century chimney-tops.

Aside from the kitchens and the infirmary, the heating-room was the only place in the Abbey where a fire could be made, by 12th-century custom. So the monks would go into that room to warm up, oil their sandals, and periodically get themselves bled.

the refectory

THE HEATING-ROOM WAS CLOSE TO THE REFECTORY and the kitchens, two sections that no longer exist at Fontenay. The old refectory was destroyed in 1745 by the monks themselves because it was about to collapse. You may return to the south gallery of the cloister to view the building's door, and to imagine the refectory that used to lie perpendicular to the cloister, as in practically all Cistercian abbeys.

If you step out into the garden and stand facing the 19th-century building (the Seguin gallery, reserved to private use), notice the gable on your right (not for visiting). This is the inner face of one of the old refectory's bays.

Beyond the cloister

At Fontenay, as at most abbeys, various other buildings stood about within the surrounding walls.

The infirmary

YOU LEAVE THE CLOSED UNIVERSE OF THE MONASTERY by a passage running along the chapter house, or by the door from the monks' room. A pretty terraced house overlooks the French garden; the roughcast mortar on the façade is still that of the 18th century. This is the infirmary, whose walls probably date from the founding of the Abbey. The monks cultivated medicinal plants near this building, most likely where the French garden lies now.

The infirmary was a world apart, set under the control of the nurse. The monastery's life was mirrored there ; masses and services were celebrated for the monks who were too ill to go into the church. Patients also had the right to eat meat. And as with the dormitory arrangements, where the lay brothers lived separated from the monks, they had their own infirmary.

The forge

NOW YOU ARE FACING A LARGE MEDIEVAL BUILDING that stretches south of the Abbey. It is the old forge, which the monks built in the late 12th century. The structure measures fifty-three meters by thirteen-and-a-half, and it is reinforced by a row of powerful two-story buttresses along the façade.

- The first chamber, to the west, is capped by four pointed vaults.
- The second, the tallest, has an upper storey. Visible at the four corners are the bases of ogive arches, which suggests that the chamber may have been vaulted.
This was probably the forge proper : Two hearths stood against the south wall; their flue openings are still visible in the masonry there.
- The third chamber, the largest, is spanned by six pointed arches. Its architecture bears some resemblance to the storeroom at Noirlac Abbey.
- The last chamber has four pointed-arch vaults, and it is thought that the Abbey's mill was located there.

One of Europe's oldest metalworking factories?

The four-chamber grouping described above has always been called a "Forge." According to Professor P. Benoît, specialist at the Sorbonne in medieval metal industry, while there is so far no proof of the existence of a true factory at Fontenay, there is a "very strong presumption." Certain facts support this near-certainty ; in the late 12th century, the Cistercians of Burgundy and Champagne were producing iron on a commercial basis, in particular at Cîteaux, Clairvaux, Pontigny and Morimont. In 1217, Eudes III, Duke of Burgundy, granted Cîteaux the right to mine ore within the Montbard castle-ward, and to harvest the firewood needed to convert it. Furthermore, researchers from "The Association for Historical and Archaeological Study of the Fontenay Forge" have recently excavated the complex network of water conduits laid beneath this abbey. The lower duct along the south side of the forge dates from the time the monks settled on the Fontenay site. It opens into a chamber that draws water laterally from a diversion of the river (which also dates from the twelfth century). The flow from that outlet is more than adequate to drive wheels down below. Lastly, sizeable mining shafts were uncovered by those same investigators in the Fontenay Forest, on a plateau overlooking the Abbey from the north. Five of the nine shafts have galleries off them. Ore taken lately from the mining sites is easily melted down in ovens (which must have been set up right there) and its iron yield is better than 64%. A mining source directly at hand, and plenty of water power for driving the tilt-hammers : The Fontenay Forge is in all likelihood one of the earliest metalworking plants in Europe.

The Residence of the commendatory Abbots

AS YOUR TOUR ENDS, to the left of Building 19 you pass before an elegant pavilion from the first half of the 18th century. This was the residence of the commendatory abbots, the new abbey chiefs who were named by the king rather than by vote of the monks, as Fontenay entered the commendation system in 1547.

The Dovecote

NEXT TO THE ABBATIAL RESIDENCE, the dovecote stands beside the path to the church. The walls of its tower are more than a meter thick, and its construction must date

from the twelfth or thirteenth century. It is a reminder that Fontenay had "pigeon rights".
A little farther along the way, two dog sculptures mark the kennel. The Duke of Burgundy hunted in the nearby Grand Jailly forests, and boarded his dogs here.

Above :
the 12ᵗʰ century
dovecote.

Left page :
Great Forge
building, 12ᵗʰ century.

The Bakery

JUST ALONGSIDE, YOU MAY ENTER THE MONKS' BAKERY, which still has its old cylindrical oven.

The outsiders' chapel

THE LONG BUILDING that now houses the bookshop and the stonework museum were probably the Chapel for Outsiders; such visitors were not permitted to enter the monastery precinct itself.
The structure dates from the 13ᵗʰ century. In the south gable is a double-bay window flanked by two other arched windows. Two matched bays open onto the lower storey. At the left of the gatehouse exit, the visitors' hostel probably stood where the present-day building does.

The Gatehouse

THE GATEHOUSE, where visitors now await the start of the tour, has an upper storey rebuilt in the 15ᵗʰ century. The section facing the inside of the Abbey was doubtless remodeled in the 17ᵗʰ century. To the right of the staircase is the watch-dog's niche and the hole in the wall he could put his head through if he wanted to show himself...

The gatehouse was a very important place in the abbeys; it marked the frontier with the outside. The doorkeeper was responsible for welcoming (and screening) everyone who came to the monastery threshold: pilgrims, travelers, merchants, but also the poor and the sick begging alms. While an abbey was a closed and protected universe, it was also in contact with the external world.

A TOUr
of the Abbey

*The Abbey's
coat of arms.*

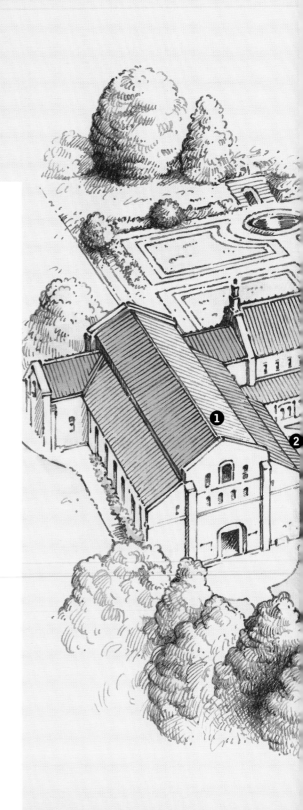

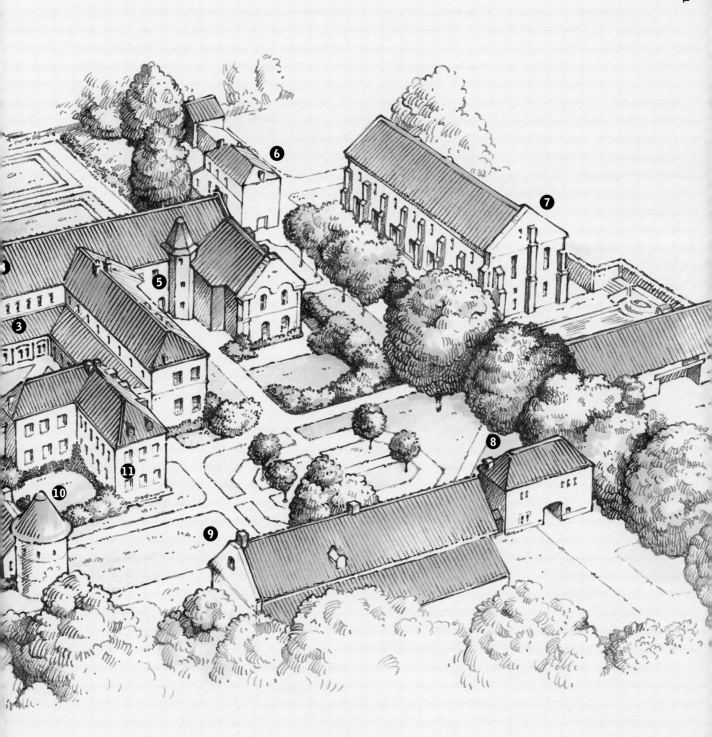

fontenay

SINCE THE REVOLUTION

The Abbey Turned into a Factory

With the French Revolution, Fontenay was sold as a National Property and turned into a paper mill. The Montgolfier family bought the Abbey in 1820 and developed the plant, which employed nearly three hundred people in the Vale by the late 19th century.

A papermill in the forge

NOW A NATIONAL PROPERTY, Fontenay was sold as real estate in April 1791. Claude Hugot, of Précy-sous-Thyll, acquired the "forementioned Bernardin abbey of Fontenay" and its domain for the sum of 78,000 francs. He installed a papermill in the forge building, and took as partner Éloi Guérin, of Paris, who bought the business from him in 1796.

FONTENAY'S HYDRAULIC SYSTEM–the millrace and the waterfall from the former forge– provided power to drive the pounding mills that turn rags to pulp for paper. Also, the Abbey's vaulted ceilings were perfectly suited to the fiber-fermentation phase. In addition, there was sufficient space for drying the paper. From the moment it was set up, the papermill in the former abbey worked at full capacity. It was the largest one in the Côte d'Or, by 1792 employing fourteen men and eight women.

The Abbey saved by industry

Above :
the church in
the papermaking
period.

IT WAS FONTENAY'S GREAT GOOD FORTUNE to have been put to immediate industrial use. In the post-Revolutionary period, with its utter lack of interest in religious heritage, the Abbey's buildings might easily have been torn down and its materials put to use else-where (as happened at Pontigny). Thus industry saved the Abbey from probable destruction.

Left page :
the Abbey
in about 1870.

ÉLOI GUÉRIN, FONTENAY'S OWNER, moved into the abbatial residence and became a figure of consequence in local life. At his death, in l820, his daughter determined to sell the property.

ÉLIE DE MONTGOLFIER, a descendant of the famous astronauts and a member of the Annonay papermaker dynasty, acquired Fontenay on October 3, 1820. The two merchants who were producing paper since Guérin's death had formed a corporation; they stayed on. But the business failed in 1829. Montgolfier decided to move onto the estate with his two sons, Raymond and Laurent, and take over production at the factory themselves.

The Montgolfiers modernize the paper plant

ÉLIE DE MONTGOLFIER was ahead of his time; he traveled a good deal and believed in modern techniques for papermaking, which in France was a highly tradition-bound industry. He installed a 20-meter paper machine in the forge building, as well as a steam boiler to heat the cast-iron rollers for drying the paper. That mechanization put the Fontenay papermill back on its feet, and many orders came in from the press industry in Paris.

IN 1838, THE PAPERMAKER SOLD FONTENAY to his son-in-law, Marc Seguin. This great scientist, the builder of railroads and inventor of suspension bridges, ordered the construction of the house that backs onto the south gallery of the cloister. Marc Seguin leased the complex to Raymond and Laurent de Montgolfier, who sped further development of the papermill. A new plant was built in the field that visitors pass as they approach the Abbey.

IN THE SECOND HALF OF THE 19TH CENTURY, the vale became a veritable industrial complex. The Montbard papermills company employed two hundred people at the Fontenay plant and another hundred-fifty at Choiseau. Workers' housing was built for the families, and one such structure from the period can still be seen, on the right in front of the gatehouse.

1903: The Fontenay factory ceases production

IN 1868, MARC SEGUIN SOLD FONTENAY back to Raymond de Montgolfier. The 1870 war had damaged the papermill, and production was interrupted for six months. In the last years of the century, the mill no longer turned a profit, despite winning a silver medal for its wrapping papers at the Universal Exposition in 1900. The steam boilers burned too much coal, and the dispersion of the production sites through the valley was a handicap. The company ended its activity in 1903.

Edouard Aynard, a wealthy Lyons banker married to Raymond's daughter Rose de Montgolfier, bought Fontenay in 1906. The industrial page in the book of Fontenay's history was turned over for good.

Portrait of a Patron

Just as Bishop Evrard of Norwich's fortune had made it possible to build Fontenay Abbey, Edouard Aynard's money paid for its huge restoration. Great art collector, banker, deputy to the National Assembly from the Rhone district, he can be seen as representative of the liberal and cultivated grand bourgeoisie of Lyon. Founder of the Textile Museum of Lyon and a member of the French Institute (Academy of Fine Arts), Edouard Aynard also calls to mind the great Florentine patrons of the Renaissance. He liked to say that he was merely the "respectful and temporary steward" of Fontenay, a maxim his descendants have taken up in their own turn.

fontenay reborn from its industrial ashes

A century of industrial activity had completely muddled the groundplan of the former Cistercian abbey. Edouard Aynard, with his son, was to bring the medieval monastery back to life by demolishing all the parasite structures related to the papermill.

A GREAT ART LOVER, the new owner had bought Fontenay as a "piece" to add to his collection of masterworks, with no intention of making the property yield a return as its previous owners had. A visionary, from the start he had to imagine the place in its medieval purity. The Lyonnais banker determined then to pull Fontenay out of the "industrial sludge" of the 19th-century papermill ; "I was caught," he said, "by the irresistible attraction of the work of art to be revived and restored." The project was a colossal one–both financially and technically.

1906-1911: The Dismantling of the Industrial Buildings

CONSIDER THE CONDITION OF THE ESTATE in 1906. Two 60-meter-tall chimney stacks rose from the north flank of the church and behind the south façade of the forge, which had been given an upper storey and two extra wings. All sorts of additions had been hooked onto the older buildings–garages, sheds, laundries. The west gallery of the cloister had gained a second storey.

FROM 1906 TO 1911, AN ENORMOUS DEMOLITION project was carried out to bring back the old medieval abbey trapped for a century in the "sludge" of the papermill. According to Lucien Bégule, who wrote the first monograph on Fontenay (1912), nearly four thousand square meters of structures were torn down.

Restoring the Interiors

MEANWHILE, EDOUARD AYNARD AND HIS SON RENÉ were eager to restore the interiors of those Abbey chambers that had been changed. The floor of the church was returned to its original level, and in removing the overlays, workers uncovered some enamel tiles and tombstones that are now reset in the church's choir.

The partitions walling off the arcades in the nave and in the chapter house were removed. The 19th-century storey atop the cloister's west gallery was taken down, and demolition proceeded on the workshops that stood in the east and north sides.

Behind the abbots' residence, the chimney... of the church

A Family Tree of Fontenay's present Owners

(a descendant of the inventors of the hot-air balloon, purchases Fontenay in 1820 and develops the papermill)

Elie de Montgolfier

Raymond de Montgolfier

Edouard Aynard

(buys Fontenay in 1906)

Rose de Montgolfier

12 children

(restores Fontenay between 1906 and 1911) **René Aynard**

(restores the dormitory in 1961) **Pierre Aynard**

(current owner, living at Fontenay since 1947) **Hubert Aynard**

François Aynard

Above and below : family photos from the 1930s.

Right page : September 1939, mobilization poster on the Fontenay plane-tree.

Rigourous principles and the refusal of replication

EDOUARD AYNARD INITIATED AND FINANCED the restoration program at Fontenay, but it was his son René, an industrialist and businessman, who truly crafted the project, and who continued the work until his death in 1943. Although the Abbey had been registered as a national Historic Monument back in 1852, René Aynard acted as his own contractor to carry out the major restorations at Fontenay.

RENÉ AYNARD'S PHILOSOPHY OF RESTORATION, inherited from his father, was governed by three cardinal principles : all restoration must be grounded on visible original traces; present-day reconstruction of a building or element that is totally vanished was forbidden (however tempting it might be, for instance, to rebuild the waterbasin in the cloister from a drawing by Viollet-le-Duc) ; and preference should always go to local materials of the same kind as those being replaced.

A vacation property

IN THE YEARS BETWEEN THE WORLD WARS, the whole extended Aynard family, with its many cousins, would spend the three summer months at Fontenay. For the children, it was a paradise of hide-and-seek and of hair-raising bike chases through the cloister arcades. A tennis court was built behind the church; there were croquet games in the nave; the children staged plays in the chapter house. "It was chateau life in an abbey," recalls Hubert Aynard. In midsummer, every habitable corner of the Abbey was taken; the residence of the commendatory abbots, the Seguin gallery, the dormitory (known as "the priory," where René Aynard lived), the infirmary and part of the upper storey of the forge.
Fontenay would become a veritable village in that season, with sometimes as many as a hundred people on the place. Evenings, after a last stroll in the cloister or a final card game, small clusters would wander in the garden by the gleam of oil lanterns.

"Knock hard several times and wait"

A FARMER MANAGED THE TWO HUNDRED HECTARES OF LAND – the cultivated fields were the ones the monks had cleared eight hundred years earlier–and a gardener took care of the kitchen plot located where the French formal garden lies now. The Fontenay stream was entrusted to a fishing club, and a groundskeeper chased off poachers. As in the time of the papermill, the Abbey was always open to visitors interested in old buildings.

IN THE LATE 1930s some five thousand persons were visiting the Abbey each year. "Knock hard several times and wait outside," said a sign on the doorway, and the watchman's wife would come out of her apartment to take visitors around Fontenay.

The Germans occupy Fontenay

ON SEPTEMBER 3, 1939, THE OUTBREAK OF WAR put an abrupt end to those happy times. The Aynard family left only for the June 1940 evacuation [the "exodus"] ordered by the French Army. A German cavalry detachment occupied Fontenay for the next year, a hundred men in all. They used the church as their stables, and built fires in the Abbey's halls to get warm. In 1941, the Aynards returned.

RENÉ AYNARD DIED IN 1943, and his son Pierre became the owner. As the Allies invaded France in June 1944, the Germans again occupied the Abbey, and the landowners joined the Resistance fighters in the Grand Jailly forest. In September 1944, Montbard was liberated and the Germans left Fontenay.

The work goes on...

The first of the family to make his permanent home at Fontenay, in 1947, Hubert Aynard, the new proprietor, gradually turned his attention to the development of tourism at the Abbey.

A small holding

AFTER THE WAR, the present proprietor had no plans for tourism at the site. Of course, the Abbey was always open to the public, but it was the farming revenues that were expected to meet the costs of conservation and upkeep at Fontenay. At the time, the property consisted of 120 hectares of woods and 80 hectares of wheatfields. Hubert Aynard also raised milk cows, and he established a fish farm in the Choiseau pond, resuming the tradition of the Cistercian monks. The operation was industrialized during the 1950s.

The purity of the water in the Fontenay creek stood as guarantee for the quality of the Abbey's trout, which became famous and were served in the best restaurants of Burgundy. In 1970, the pisciculture produced twenty tons of fish a year, and smoked trout, cured on the estate, was marketed under the name "Fontenay Trout."

The Daily Concerns of an Abbey Owner

Fontenay holds twenty thousand square meters of roofing, and structures cover an area of ten thousand square meters. The figures give some idea of the burden of maintenance required for a monument more than eight centuries old. With its classification as Historic Monument, the Abbey enjoys state subsidies for repairs, which may cover 40% of the costs.

The rest of the funding must come from the landowner. All the income from tourist admissions is reinvested in conservation. The profits from the bookstore go to balance the budget.

The roofs are damaged not only by the weather; supersonic aircraft flying too low also shake the tiles loose. Very long freezes–the temperature sometimes drops to minus 20 degrees C. at Fontenay–is devastating for the walls. The latest major work (costing about two million francs) was carried out in 1980. A study in progress at the Historic Monuments Office will determine what work should be done over the next ten years ; a third of the roofing must be restored (on the forge, the dormitory, the abbatial residence). A drastically sagging wall in the south gallery of the cloister needs investigation, and heavy masonry repairs are required in the chapter house. Apart from such major projects, there is the everyday basic maintenance : tile repair, repainting of door- and windowframes, clearing the water system and tending the garden.

The Latest Restorations

RESTORATION WORK has gone on steadily at Fontenay since 1947, always with the goal of giving the place back its original look. In 1961-63, Pierre Aynard and his son Hubert — the present owner—revived the great monks' dormitory with their decision to tear away the apartments that were obscuring it. Once it was visible again, the magnificent form of the ceiling structure was restored. In the mid-seventies, a nineteenth-century chapel in the west end of the forge was demolished and, later, the partitions closing off the various halls in the building were pulled out. The interior of the building thus regained its harmony. And now some final projects have been completed, again at the owner's instigation and under the direction of the Historic Monuments Office ; the pitched roofs of the two chapels off the church apse now follow their original design.

The Decision for Tourism

BETWEEN 1965 AND 1970, the number of visitors to Fontenay rose from 20,000 a year to 30,000. The trout-farming continued, but meanwhile the owner decided to develop the tourism operation ; he took a number of steps to bring the Abbey to public attention. A network of "Private Homes in Burgundy" was formed, and Aynard also represented the region in the national association of private owners of "Historic Homes".

World Heritage Status

THE YEAR 1981 WAS A TURNING POINT ; the Abbey was listed on UNESCO'S World Heritage list. In 1983 the proprietor decided to end the trout-farming and create first a book store, then a stonework museum, in the old outsiders' chapel.
The record of 100,000 annual visitors was broken in 1989. The farming chapter was closed for good, and Fontenay became what it is today: a true small cultural enterprise. The multilingual guides no longer have the old-time Burgundy accent, and the picturesque sign saying "Knock hard several times and wait" has vanished.

Fontenay Today : a Cultural Site

Life at the Abbey is not limited to guided tours. For the past fifty years, Fontenay has been the shooting location for many movie and television films, and has presented various other cultural events (concerts, dance, theater), notably as part of Michel Parent's "Burgundy Nights."
The closing scenes of Jean-Paul Rappeneau's "Cyrano de Bergerac" were filmed there in 1989.
Since 1997, Fontenay Abbey and the Montbard organization "Heritage and Music" have joined to present a great annual concert in the Abbey-church, with world-renowned artists (James Bowman, Mstislav Rostropovitch). And plans are afoot to make an art gallery of the second floor of the forge.

Cyrano de Bergerac (Gerard Depardieu) at Fontenay.

The working
OF IRON

Buffon's forges

Fontenay was a prominent site in the early development of iron ore by the monks. Five centuries later, Buffon determined to mine his own ore not far from the Abbey.

GEORGES-LOUIS LECLERC, COUNT DE BUFFON, the renowned naturalist of the Enlightenment born at Montbard in 1707, conducted many experiments in the smelting and working of iron ores in Burgundy.

His goal: to show that even a poor ore could be brought to produce high-quality iron. But his neighbors objected to his experiments. He therefore decided, in 1768 at the age of sixty, to exploit his discoveries and build his own blast furnaces. They were set up a few kilometers from Fontenay, at Buffon.

Within a year, iron was already being mined. In four years, the Great Forge was built. Buffon saw to everything. The mill-race dug by man-(and woman-) power to divert the Armançon River provided both for generating energy to drive the machinery and for building on a single site the full series of shops involved in the production cycle of traditional metalworks: the blast furnaces, the refinery, the slitting mill. It was the first integrated metallurgic system in the region.

Buffon's Great Forge is the model of an industrial plant from the classical period, when functional requirements were bound together with aesthetics. The whole complex, which brings French classical architecture into harmonious synthesis with Burgundy regional tradition, extends over two levels: one down in the Armançon valley for production processes, and the other higher up, for related structures.

Above :
Bust of Buffon.

Opposite :
the ceremonial
staircase of the
Great Forge.

ON THE ROCKY BLUFF, SAFE FROM THE FREQUENT FLOODING, were set those auxiliary buildings of the plant: living quarters, warehouses, supply sheds, etc.

The great courtyard is oriented east-west, with its portal facing the dovecote, so that at the summer solstice the rising sun shines through the great grillwork gate. The place looks like one of the vast farmsteads being built at the time in

"GENIUS IS ONLY A GREATER CAPACITY FOR PATIENCE."
BUFFON

the Paris Basin by other French aristocrats caught up in an agriculture craze.

Under lime trees on the left of the courtyard stands the Buffon Pavilion, the residence where the naturalist, writer, scientist and ironmaker/proprietor stayed when he came to visit his factory. In its location alongside the forge, the pavilion could hardly have been a tranquil spot, with the infernal din of the hammers pounding night and day.

ALONG THE RETAINING BANK OF THE MILL-RACE, the actual factory brings together the range of workshops.

The blast-furnace has a distinctive façade, which can be seen from the Buffon Pavilion: an arcaded front wall that looks more like a chapel than an industrial building. To give his forge still greater dazzle, so that it should measure up to its universal acclaim, Buffon endowed his blast-furnace with a feature unmatched among the forges of the period: the monumental grand staircase that descends majestically to the casting-shed, with its central flight splitting in two at midpoint to form a broad horseshoe.

The two terraces bordering the stairway allowed Buffon and his distinguished guests to look on as the metal was poured into the molds.

Buffon boasted that in his Great Forge he manufactured iron as high in quality as Swedish iron. We have proof enough of that in the grill gates of the Jardin des Plantes in Paris (the former King's Garden, where Buffon was superintendent for nearly fifty years) which he commissioned from himself.

E. D.

The façade of the Buffon Forge.

vallourec in Montbard

In the 19th century, the metallurgy industry resumed in the Montbard area : a plant was established at a few kilometers distance from Buffon's old forges.

IN THE 19TH CENTURY, charcoal-burning forges were succeeded by coke forges. The local industry joined the evolving technology. Philippe Boucy selected Montbard, well-located on transport systems, as his site for developing the new hollow-casting ("corps creux") technique.

GROUND WAS BROKEN in 1895. The Hollow-Casting Company was born. Production began two years later, with the completion of the foundry. The company lasted a brief time ; it was resold in 1899 to the Montbard Metallurgic Company (SMM), whose stock was traded on the Paris exchange.

THAT FIRM WAS THE ORIGIN OF VALLOUREC (one of France's prime manufacturers of pipe) which was established in 1957. At the present time, six Vallourec companies are operating at the Burgundy location.

A rolling mill
in the Vallourec factory.

A forest
AND A STREAM

A setting of woods and water

FONTENAY'S MANORIAL FOREST, which is part of the registered site and which forms a veritable jewel-case of green for the Abbey, is closely bound up with the monastery. It was there that S' Bernard and his men found refuge, in the heart of that valley known today as "S' Bernard's Pond." Great land-clearing labors ultimately let the Cistercians begin construction of the Abbey on that extraordinary site.

That setting of woods and ponds is intimately connected to the monks' life. It is inherent in their outlook. Water and stone, iron and wood, the Fontenay forest would, through the centuries, be a source of energy and of precious raw materials. The water from its springs would provide the hydraulic power to drive the wheels of the forge; the forest and its timber be turned to fuel; the iron from its mines be taken from the area called "Les Munières."

And later on, the forest would become a hunting ground for the monks.

Today's Fontenay Forest, six hundred hectares, is only half the thousand-hectare woodland holdings of the former Abbey's monks. Yet there are still those same tall clusters of beech and pine as before. A few plantings of spruce and pine now vary the landscape.

Troutfishing at Fontenay

THE FONTENAY STREAM IS LEASED TO A FISHING CLUB. From May to September, it is paradise to fly-fishermen playing hide-and-seek with the wild trout hidden behind the reeds and rocks. The "dry-fly" technique is considered the queen of fishing methods. There exists a great variety of artificial flies for inciting the fish to bite. The trout will not fall for crude imitations! There are spiders that mimic mayflies; "sedges" that mimic adult tricoptera; palmers that mimic houseflies or other buzzing things. The fisherman's whole craft consists in approaching as quietly as possible and then knowing how to "whip" the pole to cast the line and set the fly down gently at the target spot. The beginner who never fails to catch his hook in the tree branches will learn that fly fishing is a school for patience and humility.

The Beech, Fontenay's Tree

Its names are many : foyard, fayard, fay, fau, fou, foyaus, fagettes.
The beech tree is the main growth found at Fontenay ; it covers some seventy percent of the area. It is a tree that requires shade to germinate, and can manage on rather shallow soil like that found in the region.

> "WHAT I KNOW
> OF THE WISDOM
> OF GOD AND
> THE SCRIPTURES,
> I LEARNED IN THE WOODS
> AND THE FIELDS.
> MY ONLY TEACHERS
> ARE THE BEECHES
> AND THE OAKS."
> BERNARD OF CLAIRVAUX

"fontenay
TROUT"

Marc Meneau, of L'Espérance at Saint-Père-sous-Vézelay, confides the secrets of his recipe for trout.

ingredients
(for eight persons)

~

8 small trouts, about 180 grams each
20 grams shallots
2 cl wine vinegar
5 cl white wine
100 grams butter
Wild thyme to taste
Salt and pepper to taste
One glass cooked beet juice

8 large potatoes
Clarified butter

~

prepared by marc meneau

PREPARING THE TROUT
Lift the filets off the bone. With the patience of a monk, and tweezers, pull out any remaining small bones. Sprinkle filets with wild thyme, salt, pepper, and light olive oil; place them on a buttered plate, and chill.

PREPARING THE SAUCE
Sweat the minced shallot. Moisten with the wine vinegar and the white wine; reduce by half. Blend in the softened butter and beet juice ; season with salt, pepper, and lemon if desired. Pass your filets under the toaster grill, two minutes each side.

PREPARING THE POTATOES
Cook the potatoes in their skins ; peel them. Slice thin (5 cm), re-warm in the clarified butter.

FINISHING AND PRESENTATION
Stand three slices of potato in a rosette at the center of each plate, then arrange the two slices of very warm trout filet. Drizzle with a little sauce, and serve the rest in a pitcher.

The Pisciculture in Fontenay

The water of the Fontenay Creek is very pure, and its trout have always been renowned. According to Corbolin, "The abbots used the fish farms to make grateful reciprocation for the royal and ducal protections granted the Abbey. When a king visited Burgundy, that trout pâté awaited him at Semur or at Châtillon, and often even preceded or followed him to Dijon." The Fontenay monks held exclusive fishing rights in the vale's creek. On the eve of the Revolution, two men from Marmagne were even convicted because they had taken crayfish from the Choiseau pond.

Series editor : Evelyne Demey

Art director : Muriel Kerba
Copy Chief : Kellie Bourque
Illustration : Grimage
Engraving : SOS
Printing : SYL

Bibliography

- Corbolin, curé de Marmagne, *Monographie de l'abbaye de Fontenay, seconde fille de clairvaux,* Cîteaux, 1882.
- Lucien Bégule, *L'Abbaye de Fontenay et l'architecture cistercienne,* Lyon, 1912.
6ᵉ édition revue et corrigée par Hubert Aynard, Éditions Henri Laurens, 1994.
- Jean-François Bazin, Marie-Claude Pascal, *L'Abbaye de Fontenay,* Éditions Ouest-France, 1989.
-Patrick Boutevin, *Abbaye de Fontenay,* Éditions Gaud, 1996.
- Paul Benoît, *Un site industriel médiéval : l'abbaye de Fontenay,* Association pour l'étude historique et archéoloqique de la Forge de Fontenay, 1987.
- Denis Cailleaux, *La Restauration de l'abbaye de Fontenay (1906-1911),* Bulletin archéologique du C.T.H.S, 1987.
- Louis André, *La Papeterie des Montgolfier à Fontenay au XIXᵉ siècle,* Annales de Bourgogne, 1987.
- Léon Pressouyre, *Le Rêve cistercien,* Découvertes Gallimard, 1990.
- Georges Duby, *L'Art cistercien,* Flammarion, 1998.
- Terryl N. Kinder, *L'Europe cistercienne,* Zodiaque, 1997.
- *L'ABCdaire des Cisterciens et du monde de Cîteaux,* Flammarion-ANCR, 1998.
- Jacques Lacarrière, *La Plus Belle Aventure du monde,* Editions ANCR, 1998.
- Dom Jean Leclercq, *Saint Bernard et l'esprit cistercien,* Seuil, 1966.
- André Philibée, *Saint Bernard,* CERF, 1990.

Photographs by

Nicolas Bruant

and from

Bibliothèque de Dijon : p. 4 ; p. 11 ; p. 12 ; p. 20 b ;
Archives Fontenay / Aynard : p. 4 ; p.5 ; p. 10 ; p. 12 d ; p. 33 ; p. 37 ; p. 52-53 ; p. 40 à 46 ;
Sigma / B. Barbier : p. 4 ; p. 47 ;
Dios /Douillet : p. 7 above
Dios / Clyne : p. 7 below